California History
for Children

A handbook of short stories
from California's colorful past
Facts for teachers, children,
parents and grandparents

Edited by James Stevenson, Ph.D.

James Stevenson Publisher
1500 Oliver Road, Suite K-109
Fairfield, CA 94533
707-208-2756

First Printing: February, 1999
Second Printing: November 1999
Third Printing: March 2002
Revision: January 2006

ISBN 1-885852-12-6

Library of Congress Catalog Card Number 98-83030

Contents

California History for Children
Illustrations

Stories from California's Colorful Past

Preface
California History for Children

Several years ago we completed a period of celebration of the Gold Rush era in California and the Sesquicentennial of Statehood, during which we, as a publisher of California history books, pondered the need to present the many short stories of historic events not often written about in children's books. Children's books pay scant attention to Statehood issues, or to the lives of some of the early explorers or pioneers. Most do cover the Gold Rush and California Missions, however they overlook many exciting stories.

These short stories cover material of interest to all fans of California history, but especially to the younger student, the child who has begun the 4th grade curriculum of California history, or who has recently completed that subject. This is the group to whom this book is dedicated. In many communications, children and adults have asked how California was named, and others have asked for the words to California's state song.

In this sampler of California history one will find the answers to these questions and others such as: Who was the first European to discover California? Who named the Golden Gate?

You will find the story of the California Missions, the Donner Party and the Bear Flag Revolt, all told in a short, easy to read format. The material is adapted from the public school work of Harr Wagner with some new illustrations added to those presented by Mr. Wagner. We hope that you will find these factual stories to be as entertaining as they are informative.

James Stevenson, Ph.D.
Fairfield and Vacaville, CA

Stories from California's Colorful Past

Mission Bells
Madge Morris Wagner
Excerpt from A*t San Diego Bay*

Here first on California's soil,
Cabrillo walked the lonesome sands;
Here first the Spanish standard rose
Upon the sea-washed Western lands,

What saw they here, that fearless band,
To bless, or touch with loving hand?
Or bid them pause, to dream and stay,
Around this silent, sleeping bay?

They served, and toiled, and built, and planned,
But ever saw a promised land;
And heard its slowly rising swells
Ring joyous from their mission bells.

Time crept by those mission bells,
And back, and tied their tongues with rust,
And touched the eyelids of the priest,
And garmented his bones with dust.

In silence sleeps the bay no more -
Treasures of new wealth are found;
In its crescent-curving shore
With growing cities girded round;

No seer hath need to tell for thee,
Oh, California!
Thy daring and thy destiny.

Stories from California's Colorful Past

Juan Rodriguez Cabrillo

Juan Rodriguez Cabrillo was born in either Portugal or Spain, around 1500. He served with Conquistador Hernan Cortez. He fought for Spain against the Aztecs who lived in Mexico, then later settled in Guatemala.

By the mid-1530's Cabrillo was a leading citizen of Guatemala's main town, Santiago. On June 24, 1542 he sailed from Mexico, from Acapulco, which in those days was called Natividad. The *San Salvador* which he commanded, was the leading ship. This is called a "flagship." Three months later he arrived at a very good port. That port is known today as San Diego bay. He sailed north and west, looking at the coast with great care, especially looking for its capes and inlets.

His visit to California began on the 28th of September, 1542. Cabrillo anchored in the harbor which he called San Miguel. Sixty years later the explorer, Vizcaino, changed the name to San Diego.

Cabrillo visited the islands of Santa Cruz, Catalina, and San Clemente. He died January 3, 1543 and was probably buried on San Miguel Island. Bartolome Ferrelo, his chief pilot, took command of the expedition. To Cabrillo belongs the honor of being the first European to reach the shores of California.

The man who reported on the voyage wrote: "A wind blew from the west-southwest and from the southwest, but the port being good, they felt nothing," because the harbor was so protected.

Cabrillo remained in the harbor six days. The Indians came down to the shore, and looked at the ship. At first they were very timid. One night, when the men were fishing, the Indians shot arrows at them, and wounded three. The sailors were very careful after this.

The Indians told Cabrillo that away from the ocean, there were men dressed like the Spaniards. He took great interest in the natives, and was said to have treated them kindly. The sailors did not want to leave

Cabrillo landing at San Diego Bay

San Diego Bay, because it was such a good harbor, but Cabrillo was anxious to sail northward.

The man who wrote the record of the places to which Cabrillo sailed in his voyage was not very exact when he wrote about the places they visited. So the reader is not always sure of the ports he meant. It is certain, however, that he sailed to San Pedro, Santa Monica and Santa Barbara. Cabrillo gave long names to these places, but they are not the ones now on the maps.

At Santa Barbara Cabrillo found some natives who wore their hair long. They had it fixed up with some strings with flint, bone, and wooden daggers. They caught fish, and ate them raw. They also had good canoes, and in many ways had a better life than other Indians.

Cabrillo then sailed farther north. His ship drifted northwestward with the wind; the weather was pleasant, the coast rough, without harbors, and off in the distance lofty mountains were covered with snow.

One morning at dawn, as the sun sowed its path of gold across the brown hills to the sea, he saw a point of land covered with pines. He called it the Cape of the Pines. Then he sailed on and on, past the Golden Gate and the great harbor within, to Point Reyes.

History says he turned southward and "descended under lofty snow-capped mountains so near that they seemed about to fall on them." The ship anchored in a little harbor at San Miguel Island, near

Santa Barbara. One day Cabrillo fell and broke his arm. He was not careful with it, and it brought on an illness which resulted in his death, January 3, 1543. His dying words were said to be, "Sail northwards, at all hazards."

No trace of his grave can be found; no stone marks the spot where his body rests. He did not seem to have the pirate's heart, like Balboa, Drake, Pizarro, and so many other explorers who made voyages to the Pacific.

The books do not contain long accounts of his deeds; yet his services to the world will not be forgotten. In 1937, the Cabrillo Civic Clubs of California, a statewide Portuguese group, erected a monument which overlooks San Miguel Harbor in honor of Cabrillo who made the first voyage to California.

Sir Francis Drake, the Englishman

Sir Francis Drake was a great sailor. Some of his adventures were very dangerous and exciting.

He was born in Devonshire, England, in a cottage on the banks of the Tavy. His father was a yeoman, and he had twelve sons.

While traveling about young Francis heard of the exploits of his cousin, John Hawkins and stories of the New World. He fitted out a vessel intending to act as a pirate on behalf of England. He sailed about in the West Indies. In 1567, he plundered the town of Nombre de Dios. He crossed the Isthmus of Darien, saw the Pacific Ocean, and returned to England laden with booty, a successful sea-rover. On behalf of Queen Elizabeth, Drake sailed for the Pacific. He raided the Spanish towns on the coasts of Chile and Peru. Hoping to find a passage back to the Atlantic, he sailed north. He anchored near Point Reyes, and took formal possession of the country in the name of the Queen of England. He then sailed across the Pacific, arriving at Plymouth on September 26, 1580.

He was Vice-Admiral of the fleet which destroyed the naval supremacy of the Spanish Armada.

Drake's story began when, as a young man, he met a neighbor who owned a little ship called a bark. This sea captain liked Drake and made him a mate on his ship for several voyages. On one of these voyages the old man died and left his ship to young Francis.

Not much later, Drake's cousin John Hawkins asked him to sail with him to the New World. Hawkins told him about the profits to be made in trade, and of the chances to get gold. The English and Spanish were at war. Drake thought it was justified to attack Spanish ships and Spanish towns, and to take all the gold that he could find. He secured so much gold and captured so many ships that he became a great hero to the English people.

His men landed at Darien, where Balboa had been before. Drake heard stories from the Indians of how the Spanish brought rich treasures from Peru across the Isthmus. He decided to capture the Spaniards and rob them of their gold.

Then, like Balboa, he wanted to see the "Great Water," the Pacific Ocean. Until then, he had sailed on the Atlantic Ocean. After traveling twelve days he came to the top of a hill. His Indian guide told him to climb a tree and he could see the Southern Ocean.

He looked out through the leafy branches of the tree, and beheld the smooth waters of the Pacific. He is said to have asked God to give him life and heart to sail an English ship upon the unknown sea.

The view of the Pacific made him feel that he would attain wealth and glory for England. His active mind formed many plans, all with the goal of continuing his attack on the far-flung empire of his enemy, rich and proud Spain.

At Panama he captured a mule train loaded with bars of gold and other treasures. After many trials, he again reached the Atlantic Ocean and sailed for England.

The news of his adventures and of his gold soon spread through the countryside. It was on Sunday, the 9th of August, 1573, that Drake landed in Plymouth harbor.

He was now a rich man. After giving money to all his relatives, he still had plenty to engage in new enterprises. He wanted to sail to the Pacific. One day the queen sent for him, and made him a present of a beautiful sword, and she let Drake know that she wanted him to make the trip.

He soon had a fleet of five vessels. Late in the year 1577, the gallant fleet sailed toward the setting sun.

Some time later, after many adventures, Drake sailed through the Straits of Magellan, on the Golden Hind, and saw the cape which stood at the outlet to the Pacific.

He cast anchor at the side of some lofty cliffs and went ashore. He went to the highest cliff, and going to the outer edge, he flung his arms toward the sea.

When he returned to the golden Hind, one of the men asked him where he had been. Drake replied with a proud smile: "I have been farther south than any man living." Drake left Cape Horn, and sailed northward.

All of his ships, save one, either met with disaster or deserted. So the Golden Hind sailed alone.

It followed the west coast all the way from Cape Horn to Oregon. He believed that he could find a northern passage to the Atlantic. On his way northward he stopped at coastal towns, in order to fight the Spanish, and secure gold, silver and food. Drake had with him, on the Golden Hind, a chaplain by the name of Fletcher. This man kept a record of the voyage. He tells in his report that the snow and ice could be seen on the mountains along the coast, and that the weather was so cold that Drake gave up his northern trip and returned south.

It was in June that Drake found a harbor. Some say that it was the Bay of San Francisco. But is more than likely that he passed by the Golden Gate, not dreaming that within its portals was one of the finest harbors in the world.

As he sailed south, just before reaching San Francisco, he anchored at what is known as Drake's Bay near Point Reyes. The Indians came down to the ship, and treated the sailors very kindly, regarding them with awe. The ships remained over one month at this place. They were repaired, and a new supply of water and food were secured.

Chaplain Fletcher held the first church services in California. Drake made a journey inland and saw fat deer and thousands of strange little animals that had tails like rats and paws like moles. The people ate them, and the kings had holiday coats made of their skins. All this is described in Fletcher's quaint old English that would be hard for the modern student to read.

Drake named all of California New Albion - first, because it had so many white banks and cliffs, and secondly, because Albion was the name often applied to old England.

Then he sailed west, and sailed and sailed, till

he reached England. He had gone around the world in two years and ten months, and had secured gold and disabled many Spanish ships.

Queen Elizabeth visited him and dined with him aboard the Golden Hind. The queen took his sword and said: "This sword, Drake, might still serve thee. Thou hast carried it around the globe; but ere we return it to thee, it must render us a service." Gently tapping Drake on the shoulder, she said, in a clear voice: "Rise, Sir Francis Drake."

He was now a knight. He had sailed around the globe. He had defied danger in every form. He had dealt terrible blows to the Spaniards. He had made numerous discoveries. He had returned rich, a conqueror, a pioneer. His exploits thrilled the people.

He continued to fight the Spaniards for some years, winning new laurels. King Philip of Spain sent to Queen Elizabeth the Latin verse, which translated reads thus:

"These to you are our commands:
Send no help to the Netherlands.
Of the treasures took by Drake,
Restitution you must make."

In reply, Drake fought the Spanish Armada, and continued to take treasures. He then returned to the field of his first success, and attempted to capture Panama. His men died by the score with fever. He was also taken sick; and one morning in January, in 1596, he arose to go on deck, but fell back and died, surrounded by his men, and he was buried beneath the waters that he loved so well. Drake died at Nombre de Dios.

The Golden Hind was ordered preserved. It was kept for one hundred years, but it has long since decayed. A chair made from its timbers was given by Charles II to Oxford University, and it may be seen yet - a memento of the first English ship to touch California's shores, and of its bold captain, Sir Francis Drake, the sea-king of Devon.

(Note: A Prayer-Book Cross in Golden Gate Park, gift of G. W. Childs, was erected in honor of Drake's voyage to California.)

Stories from California's Colorful Past

The March of Portola

The trip overland of Don Gaspar de Portola from San Blas, in Lower California, to the Bay of San Francisco was extremely difficult. His party faced illness, earthquakes and starvation. This is the story of their heroic trip.

In the 1700s the king of Spain was afraid the Russians would come down from the north and take California. To fortify the coast of California he sent men from Mexico City.

As a part of their expedition they had two ships at La Paz, the *San Antonio* and the *San Carlos*. These two ships were loaded, and soon set sail for the Bays of San Diego and Monterey.

The *San Carlos* was the first ship to enter through the Golden Gate into the Bay of San Francisco. Portola decided to lead the march overland. Among the men at San Blas were Ortega, Father Junipero Serra, Father Crespi, Costanxo, engineer, and Prat, a physician. Portola and his men started from San Blas on May 5, 1769. He traveled over two hundred miles to the Bay of San Diego.

It was a dreary journey. As they approached San Diego Bay the native Indians came out to meet them, and begged from Serra his robe, and took from Portola everything he wore. The Indians had Serra show them his glasses. They were a curiosity, and caused him a lot of trouble before he could get them back. The trip took forty-five days. They found that those who had come by sea on the *San Carlos* had camped near where "Old Town" San Diego is now located. They greeted with joy Portola and his men and the 163 mules carrying provisions. The *San Antonio* returned to San Blas to tell the story of the trip, and the *San Carlos*, with Captain Vila, remained at San Diego because so many sailors had died from sickness that he could not continue to Monterey.

At San Diego, Portola left the sick under the faithful Doctor Prat, and on July 14th started to March to Monterey. On July 16, 1769, Junipero Serra founded the San Diego Mission, the first one in California. Of the forty people Portola left behind, eight soldiers, four sailors, one servant and eighteen Indians died.

Among the people that Portola took with him was Pedro Amador after whom Amador County is named; Ortega, pathfinder and discoverer of the Golden Gate and the San Francisco Bay; Alvarado, grandfather of Governor Alvarado of California; Carrillo, afterwards commander at Monterey, Santa Clara and San Diego, and founder of the celebrated Spanish family in California. Portola had fitted out a small ship, called the *San Jose*, and loaded it with supplies for Monterey. He was however, a careful man, and for fear it would be lost at sea, he took with him one hundred mules laden with provisions. This was fortunate, because the ship *San Jose was* lost at sea.

It was an interesting group of men starting to tramp over 500 miles, without roads, trails or paths. How different the trip today from San Diego to the Bay of San Francisco! Here is the way Portola started out. (You may ask how do we know this? Why, father Crespi kept a diary, and he wrote everything down that happened each day.) At the head rode Fages, a commander; Costanxo, the engineer; two priests, and six others. Then came Indians, with spades and axes. These were followed by Pack mules in four sections; the last was the rear guard, with Captain Rivera and Governor Portola. Each soldier had defensive weapons; for instance his arms were wrapped with leather, so that the Indian's spears and arrows could not hurt him, and then a leather apron that fell on each side of the horse over his legs, to protect them when riding through the brush. Each soldier carried a lance a sword and a short musket. The men were fine horsemen and most were good soldiers. They traveled very slowly, not over five or six miles per day. The greatest difficulty was with the horses. It is said that a coyote, or fox, or even wild birds would frighten the horses, so that they would run away.

The trip was along what is now known as El Camino Real, the King's Highway. It took them four days to reach San Luis Rey, where the mission now is. They rested four days at San Juan Capistrano. On the 28th of July they reached the Santa Ana River, and experienced a terrible earthquake. They crossed the Los Angles River where the City of Los Angeles now stands, and gave it its name. The city itself was not founded until 1781, when the full name, Nuestra Seňora La Reina de Los Angeles (Our Lady the Queen of the Angels) was given to it. They gave the San Fernando Valley the pretty name of "Valley of St. Catherine of the Oaks." Portola crossed another river where Camulos now is, and named it Santa Clara, in honor of the Saint whose day they celebrated on August 12th. Then they marched on and on, across many rivers, and over mountains. The Indians in the rancherias welcomed them, and gave them food, and showed them how they made boats and implements of various kinds. They passed on through where Santa Barbara now is and on to San Luis Obispo. Here were many Indians. Their big chief had a tumor on his neck and the men called him and the place El Buchon. Father Crespi did not like the name, but Point Buchon and Mount Buchon, "Bald Knob," shows how names will stick.

The men were taken sick and their way to the Salinas Valley was difficult. Many of the men were afflicted with scurvy, a disease brought on by not eating enough vegetables and fruit. On the last day of September the men halted near the mouth of the Salinas River, within sound of the ocean, but could not see it. Portola now sent out scouts to look for the Bay of Monterey; but after a long search, and seeing the sand dunes, and the pines, failed to recognize the bay.

A council was called; Portola told of the shortness of provisions, and the danger of winter coming on, so that all might perish. Costanxo said they must travel farther north. Rivera thought they should find a place to camp. If Monterey was not found, they would discover some other place where they could settle. So Portola determined to put his trust in God, and move on. Sixteen of the men were so sick they had to be lifted on and off the horses. The march was slow and painful. They came to a river where the Indians killed an eagle with wings that reached seven feet four inches from tip to tip. Father Crespi called the river Santa Ana, but the people called it Pajaro, "The bird." On the 17th of October they passed through the section where is now located the beautiful town of Santa Cruz. At Waddell Creek both Portola and Rivera were taken sick. At San Gregorio it began to rain, and all were taken sick, but strange to say, the new ailments seemed to relieve the scurvy, and they were able to press forward. They marched through Half Moon Bay, and up along the coast, and reached the foot of Montara Mountains on October 30th. The site of the camp is about a mile north of Montara Light House. They named the camp El Rincon de las Almejas, on account of the mussels and other shellfish found there. Ortega and his men sere sent out to find a way over the mountains. In a few days Ortega returned and told of seeing land as far as the eye could reach. Ortega was the first white man to see the Golden Gate, and the Bay of San Francisco, which has become so famous in song and story and in the commercial life of the West.

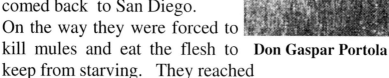

Portola and his men now crossed into the San Pedro Valley, marched over to the bay side, and camped again near the site of Stanford University. After many hardships, Portola, with his companions, were welcomed back to San Diego. On the way they were forced to kill mules and eat the flesh to keep from starving. They reached

Don Gaspar Portola

San Diego on January 18th, and reported that they searched for Monterey Bay in vain. After resting until April 17, 1770, Portola set out again for the Bay of Monterey. On May 24th they camped on the shores of Monterey Bay. Portola, Fages and Father Crespi noted the calm and placid water, the seals, and spouting whales, and all agreed: "This is the port of Monterey. It is as reported by Vizcaino." (Vizcaino discovered the Bay of Monterey in 1602 and sent a glowing account of it to the King of Spain.)

On the 3rd of June, 1770, under the shelter of the branches of an oak tree, Portola, Serra, Crespi and the soldiers met and established a presidio and a Mission. Portola, the first Governor of California, in the name of the King of Spain, took possession of the country, and thus was established the first presidio and Carmel, the second mission in California.

On July 9, 1770, Portola sailed for Mexico. He afterwards became Governor of Puebla, Mexico, and California knew him no more.

Stories from California's Colorful Past

The Story of the Missions

San Diego de Alcala

For generations, the planting of the Franciscan mission crosses in California has been called a heroic tale. In the most beautiful places from San Diego to San Francisco, Junipero Serra and his followers built missions. After the passage of more than two hundred years, they stand as landmarks of the dedication of the earliest pioneers.

The founders, in the selection of sites, found beautiful locations, where they created a style of architecture that is the basis for many of our most attractive modern buildings.

Pala Mission (Assistencia)

The mission buildings have the color and atmosphere of California. They seem to have grown up out of the brown soil. The soft dove-color of the adobe walls, the red-brown tiles of the roof, the olive leaves on the trees, the violet haze of the distant mountains, the tawny hue of the hills, all harmonize with each other.

It was at noon on July 1, 1769, that Junipero Serra stood on the mesa above San Diego Bay. It is said that as he looked out across the soft wind-dimpled ocean all about him, his soul was filled with delight, and he stooped, took a golden poppy, touched it with his lips, and exclaimed: "Copa de oro! The cup of gold! The Holy Grail! I have found it!"

Junipero Serra, whose name was José Miguel before he devoted himself to the church, had walked all the way from Mexico City to San Diego. The ship San Carlos had sailed from San Blas, and entered the harbor before the arrival of Junipero Serra and his companions. The journey overland was hard on Junipero because of a painful affliction of his foot.

He asked one of the men for a remedy for the ailment. The man replied: "I know no remedy; I am no surgeon; I can only cure the sores of beasts."

"Well, son," replied Junipero, "treat me as a beast." The man smiled at the request. He took some tallow, mashed it between two stones, mixed some herbs with it, and applied the medicine. The relief was almost immediate.

Carmel Mission

On July 14, 1769, Portola, Father Crespi and about sixty others started northward overland to Monterey, in accordance with instructions of Charles III, King of Spain. Junipero Serra at once began the work of his life. On July 16th - the anniversary of the victoryof the Spaniards over the Moors in 1212 - he erected a cross near where twin palms later stood in San Diego. Mass was celebrated. The natives looked on, and across their faces crept an expression on wonder.

One night the Indians, who were very fond of cloth, cut out a piece of the sails from the San Carlos. They would not eat the food of the Spaniards, for fear of sickness. This was fortunate for the Spaniards, as their supply was limited.

Junipero did not succeed in converting the Indians at first. Their little group was attacked one night. Jose Maria, a servant, was killed, and several others were wounded. The mission was moved in 1774 to a spot on the San Diego River, about five miles from the bay. Here palm-trees were planted, an olive orchard started, and ground cultivated.

San Gabriel Mission

On November 4, 1775, eight hundred Indians attacked the mission. Father Louis Jayme and several others were killed. The mission was burned. The few soldiers, aided by the settlers, fought bravely. In the morning the Indians picked up their dead and wounded, and marched away, and never renewed the attack.

San Luis Obispo Mission

Junipero Serra sailed for Monterey on April 16, 1770, to build a Mission. Portola, Father Crespi, and companions had made an overland journey for the purpose, but had failed to find the port mentioned by Vizcaino in 1602.

Junipero Serra succeeded in finding an immense circuit of smooth water, full of sea-lions and deep enough for whales. He landed, and on the morning of June 3, 1770, claimed possession of the place.

Under an oak tree an alter was raised, the bells were hung, and celebration was begun with loud and vigorous chimes. Junipero, in alb and stole, asked the blessing of heaven on their work. A great cross was erected.

Santa Clara Mission

Santa Barbara Mission

The famous port of Monterey was in possession of Spain, and the royal flag floated in this remote region - the Indians watched it curiously.

The mission was changed from the beach in 1771 to its present location. The beautiful wild roses, the roses of Castile, grew all about it. The Monterey cypress, the forest of pines, the Carmel River, the quiet, crescent-shaped bay marked it as a beautiful spot.

At this place Junipero Serra welcomed new arrivals, and the Indians began to come to the missions. The establishment of missions at San Luis, San Gabriel, San Juan Capistrano, San Luis Rey, Pala, Santa Barbara, San Francisco, and other places went on with great rapidity.

When the news of the conquest of California reached Old and New Spain, the bells of the cathedrals rang in tune with the mission bells of San Diego, Monterey and San Gabriel.

The missions were founded by the Order known as Franciscans. Junipero asked of Galvez: "Is St Francis to have no mission?" "Let him show us his port and he shall have one," was the reply. The port was found and San Francisco bay is named in honor of St. Francis, who devoted his life to unselfish service.

The same years that witnessed the missionary conquest of California by Spain saw a Revolution and struggle for independence on the Atlantic coast.

The missionary work and interests of Spain were well advanced by Junipero Serra. In August 1784, he sent a letter of eternal farewell to the Franciscans, and prepared for death. On August the 28th, he took leave of his old friend, Palou, and went to sleep. The mission bells tolled mournfully. The people covered his coffin with flowers, and touched this body with medals and rosaries. His garments were taken as relics. He was buried at San Carlos.

San Francisco de Asis (Mission Dolores

"He ended his laborious life," says Father Palou, "at the age of seventy years nine months and four days. Eight missions were established and 5,800 Indians were confirmed as the result of his labors in Upper California."

This much was accomplished with great hardship. He limped from mission to mission, at times passing sleepless nights listening to the howls of the coyotes. He was sometimes in danger of an attack from unfriendly Indians. The food was poor, clothing was scant, and his shelter frequently a gnarled oak. Many feel that Junipero Serra followed the paths of the saints and martyrs - the ideals of his sickly boyhood. His work belonged to a pioneer age.

The tourist of today finds a reviving interest in the old buildings with their restored adobe walls, the wide corridors, and the spirits of the many dedicated "neophytes," the Indian converts, that kept the missions running. At the turn of the century, around 1900, almost all the missions had crumbling adobe walls, with broken tiles, cracked bells. For at least one, it was difficult to make out the outlines of where the buildings had stood. The work of the future will include caring for these invaluable reminders of our unique past.

Founding dates
Franciscan Missions of California

San Diego, in San Diego County, July 16, 1769

San Carlos de Monterey (or Carmel Mission) Monterey County, June 3, 1770

San Antonio de Padua, Monterey County, July 14, 1771

San Gabriel Arcangel, Los Angeles County, September 8, 1771

San Luis Obispo, San Luis Obispo County, September 1, 1772

San Francisco de Asis, (Dolores), San Francisco County, October 9, 1776

San Juan Capistrano, Orange County, November 1, 1776

Santa Clara, Santa Clara County, January 18, 1777

San Buena Ventura, Ventura County, March 31, 1782

Santa Barbara, Santa Barbara County, December 4, 1786

La Purisima Concepcion, Santa Barbara County, December 8, 1787

Santa Cruz, Santa Cruz County, August 28, 1791

La Soledad, Monterey County, October 9, 1791

San Jose, Alameda County, June 11, 1797

San Juan Bautista, San Benito County, June 24, 1797

San Miguel Arcangel, San Luis Obispo County, July 25, 1797

San Fernando, Los Angeles County, September 8, 1797

San Luis Rey, San Diego County, June 13, 1798

Santa Ynez, Santa Barbara County, September 17, 1804

San Rafael Arcangel, Marin County, December 18, 1817

San Francisco Solano, Sonoma County, August 25, 1823

Stories from California's Colorful Past

The First Ship to Enter the Golden Gate

The ship *San Carlos* was the first to sail through the Golden Gate into the harbor of San Francisco. Drake, Cabrillo, Vizcaino, had all drifted by the bay locked in among the hills.

The Bay of San Francisco was first discovered by Portola and his land party, who were looking for the Bay of Monterey. The date was November 2, 1769, over two hundred years after Drake and Cabrillo had sailed along the coast of California.

It was not, however, until August 5, 1775, that a ship entered the narrow straits. The *San Carlos* left Monterey under instructions to sail to the port of San Francisco and make a survey.

Ayala, the commander, set sail. The ship crept cautiously along the shore. It was nine days before the men on the ship saw the seal rocks and heard the sea-lions. A launch was sent ahead to explore the narrow passage, now known as the Golden Gate. The men in the little boat sailed in against the fog that mantled the hills on either side. Ayala followed with his ship. At night he anchored in the bay, having safely passed through the straits.

The next morning the ship *San Carlos* was moored at an island, now called Angel Island. It was a delightful place. The picturesque surroundings, the springs of pure water, the chaparral, coves, and pebbly beach made it very inviting to the sailors.

The launch was used in sailing about the main

body of the bay and along its outstretched arms, the rivers, San Pablo and the smaller bays.

At Mission Bay, now filled up and built over, they saw three Indians, who were weeping, or making noises resembling crying, and for this reason the cove was named the "Cove of the Weepers."

A cross had been planted by the land party a few years before on the sand dunes of Point Lobos. At its foot Ayala ordered two letters deposited, one describing his successful entrance to, and survey of the Bay of San Francisco, the other giving notice of his return to Monterey, and asking that if the land party, which he expected, should arrive, to build a fire in sight of Angel Island. The party arrived, the fire was lighted, but no response came back.

These men were camped by the side of al lake, and gave it the name which it bears to this day - Lake Merced - in honor of "Our Lady of Mercy."

Ayala sending boat ahead in San Francisco Bay

The ship *San Carlos* had remained for forty days in the Bay of San Francisco. It had taken possession, Ayala reported, of the best port of Spain. It now sailed out of the harbor and down to Monterey.

Since that time over two hundred years ago, when Ayala first to entered the Bay, thousands of ships have sailed in and out through the Golden Gate. Flags of every nation have been wafted to the breezes of the bay. The gate stands well guarded, but the red white and blue of "Old Glory" now floats over the Presidio as a welcome rather than as a military menace.

The Story of the Donner Party

The covered wagons were packed with food, goods and articles useful in the life of the early pioneer. The oxen were yoked, and stood lazily waiting the driver's order. The children had said goodbye, and, as they climbed up on the wagons, shouted, "Ho! for California!"

Then the heavy wagons started, and the Donner party began the long, perilous journey toward the pacific. It was early in April, 1846, that George and Jacob Donner and James F. Reed formed the train which was to cross the plains. The journey began with bright hopes. It was known that the roads were difficult; that Indians might attack them; that great deserts would have to be crossed, and roads would have to be found or constructed over rough mountains.

These were the days of hardy men and women. Fathers and mothers were full of courage; lovers were full of hope; children were full of glee. The bleaching bones of cattle, and here and there a rude cross over a newly made mound, along the emigrant road, did not change their courage, hope or joy.

Fair, young California was before these people, its rich valleys, its pine-clad Sierra, its rivers and matchless sea.

After the Donner party left Independence, Missouri, it was joined by others, until it contained between two and three hundred wagons, and was, when in motion, two miles in length. The great train succeeded in reaching Fort Bridger, a trading post, without much trouble.

On one occasion, Mary Graves, a beautiful young lady, was riding on horseback with her brother. They were in the rear of the train. A band of Sioux Indians fell in love with the maiden, and offered to purchase her; but the brother was not willing to sell. One of the Indians seized the bridle of the girl's horse, and attempted to capture her. The brother leveled his rifle at the him, and he promptly gave a war-whoop and rode away.

At another place a division arose among the emigrants; some wanted to rest the stock and hunt buffaloes, and secure a larger supply of meat to be made into jerky. Others wanted to go on, for fear the grass would be eaten off by the stock of other trains. It was decided to go forward.

At Fort Bridger, the Donner party chose a new route, called the "Hastings Cut-off." Those who went by the old route reached California in safety.

The trials of the Donner party now began in earnest. Instead of reaching Salt Lake in one week, it was over thirty days, and the stock and men were exhausted. The beautiful Salt Lake Valley, however, filled them with joy, and all hoped for a peaceful, prosperous journey to California.

In crossing the Great Salt Lake Desert severe

hardships were endured. The suffering of the stock for water was great. Some teamsters unhitched the oxen from Jacob Reed's wagons, and drove them ahead for water. The desert mirage deceived the oxen and even the men, and the cattle rushed off into the pathless desert and never returned. The men went tramping through the sand and over the sage brush, calling, "Co, Boss. Co-o-o Bo-bosss! -- Soo-ok, Jer-ry -- Soo-oksook, Jerry!" No answer came. The loneliness of the desert was increased as the sound of their voices died away in the vast solitude. Reed was forced to cache the goods in his wagons and proceed with an ox and a cow. While the party was camped on the edge of the desert, it was made known that the provisions would not last until California was reached.

The group decided to send two men ahead to secure provisions and return. C.T. Stanton and William McCutcheon decided to go. A tearful farewell was taken, and the two brave men rode out on the dim trail for California. They carried letters to Captain Sutter of Sutter's Fort.

At Gravelly Ford, on the Humboldt River, a tragedy occurred. In trying to ascend a hill where it was required to hitch five or six yoke of oxen to a wagon, Reed and a popular young man by the name of John Snyder, became engaged in a fierce quarrel.

C.V. McGlashan gives this account of the affray: "When Reed saw that trouble was likely to occur, he said something about waiting until they go up the A

J.F. Reed

hill, and settle the matter afterwards. Snyder, who took this a threat, replied, "we will settle it now." He struck Reed a blow on the head with the butt-end of his heavy whipstock. The blow was followed in rapid succession by a second and a third.

As the third stroke descended, Mrs. Reed ran between her husband and the furious man, hoping to prevent the blow. Each time the whipstock descended on Reed's head it cut deep gashes. He was dazed and stunned by the terrific force of the blows. He saw the cruel whipstock uplifted, and knew that his wife was in danger, who only had time to cry, "John! John!" When down came the stroke full upon Mrs. Reed's head and shoulders. The next instant John Snyder was staggering speechless and death-stricken. Patrick Breen came up

Mrs. Margaret Reed

and Snyder said: "Uncle, I am dead." Reed's knife had entered his lung. Snyder's death fell like a thunderbolt on the Donner Party."

Reed was banished from the train. At first he refused to go, but the feeling against him was so strong that he yielded to the pleadings of is wife and daughter. He was to go without provisions or even a gun; but his twelve-year old daughter, Virginia, supplied them.

As the train moved forward, Mrs. Reed and Virginia would look at every little camping place for a message from him. He rode toward California, and when he succeeded in killing geese or ducks, he would spread the feathers about in such a way that it would be a message to his family, and sometimes would leave letters pinned to the sage brush.

The day came when they found no message, no letter, or trace of the father. Was he dead? Had he starved? Had the Indians killed him?

Mrs. Reed grew pale and worried. Then she knew that if she died her children might perish. With a brave heart she roused herself, and with noble devotion cared for her children. (Mr. Reed reached California, and returned to Donner Lake to rescue his family and aid the others. He lived at San Jose many years.)

Near the town of Wadsworth, Nevada, Stanton who had been sent on ahead, returned from Sutter's Fort with provisions. He brought seven mules, five of which were loaded with dried beef and flour. If Stanton had not brought these provisions, the whole "At Prosser Creek, three miles below Truckee, they found themselves encompassed with six inches of snow. On the summits the snow was from two to five feet in depth. This was October 28, 1846. Almost a month earlier than usual, the Sierra had donned its mantle of ice and snow.

"The party were prisoners. All was consternation. The wildest confusion prevailed. In their eagerness, many went off in advance of the main train. There was little concerted action or harmony of plan. All did not arrive at Donner Lake the same day. Some wagons and families did not reach the lake until the 31st day of October; some never went farther than Prosser Creek, while others on the evening of the 29th, struggled through the snow, and reached the foot of the precipitous cliff between the summit and the upper end of the lake. Here, baffled, wearied and disheartened, they turned back to the foot of the lake."

Several attempts were made to cross the mountains, but without success. Realizing that the winter must be passed in the mountains, arrangements were made for food, by killing the cattle and building shelters. The following is a description of the Breen cabin:

It was built of pine saplings, and roofed with pine brush and rawhides. It was twelve by fourteen feet, and seven or eight feet high, with a chimney in one end, built "Western style." One opening through which light, air and the occupants passed, served as a window and door. Two days were spent in its construction.

Patrick Dolan, a brave, generous Irishman, gave all of his food to the Reed family, and started with C.T. Stanton and thirteen others to cross the Sierra on foot.

Before they left, one man had already died of starvation. Matters were desperate. The party only dared take six days rations. The first day the party traveled four miles, the next six.

They crossed the summit. The camp of the party was no longer visible. They were alone among the high snow-peaked battlements of the Sierra. The situation was terrible. The great snowshoes exhausted them. The heroic Stanton became so blind that it was difficult for him to proceed. The agony of blindness wrung no cry from his lips. He could no longer keep up with the rest of the company.

One evening he staggered into camp, long after the others had finished their pitiful supper. He said little. In the silence of his heart he know he had reached the end of his journey. In the morning someone said kindly, "Are you coming?"

"Yes, I am coming soon." These were his last words. He died alone, amid the snow of the High Sierra.

A terrible storm arose. The group was without food. Unless they had something to eat they would all die. For this group, to live meant to consume the flesh of those who, in their weakened state, had died.

Of the original 87 in the party and two who joined the train in Nevada for a total of 89, there were only 48 survivors.

The generous Patrick Dolan died; the group struggled on until they came to an Indian Rancheria. It is said that the Indian women cried with grief at the pitiful spectacle of the starved men and women, and those who had survived under these impossible conditions. They gave them bread made from acorns, and the Indians were very kind to them. But the acorn bread did not strengthen them. They were now in full view of the Sacramento Valley, in all its beauty and loveliness, and yet were near death!

At last one, stronger than the others, went on ahead to Johnson's Ranch, and sent back food to the others. Of the fifteen who had started from Donner Lake, only seven lived to reach Johnson's Ranch.

Word reached Sutter's Fort that men, women and children were starving at the lake, and Captain Sutter sent a relief party at once.

The people who camped at the lake suffered the pangs of starvation. One of the survivors, writing said: "The families shared with one another as long as they had anything to share. Each one's portion was very small. The hides were boiled, and the bones were browned and eaten. We tried to eat a decayed buffalo robe. But it was too tough, and there was no nourishment in it. Some of the few mice that came into camp were caught and eaten.

"Some days we could not keep a fire, and many times, during both days and nights, snow was shoveled from off our tent and from around it, that we might not be buried alive. Mother remarked one day that is had been two weeks that our beds and the clothing upon our bodies had been wet.

"Two of my sisters and myself spent some days at Keseberg's cabin. The first morning we were there they shoveled the snow from our bed before we could get up.

"Very few can believe it possible for human beings to live and suffer the exposure and hardships endured there."

Quoting again from Mr. McGlashan, this touching account of Christmas on Donner Lake is given:

"What a desolate Christmas morning that was for the snowbound victims! All were starving. Something to eat, something to satisfy the terrible cravings of appetite, was the constant wish of all. Sometimes the wishes were expressed aloud, but more frequently a gloomy silence prevailed. When anything was audibly wished for, it was invariably something whose size was proportional to their hunger. They never wished for a meal or a mouthful, but for a barrelful, a wagon-load, a houseful, or a storehouseful.

"On Christmas Eve the children spoke in low subdued tones of the visits Santa Claus used to make to them before they started across the plains. Now they knew that no Santa Claus would find them in the pathless depths of snow.

"One family, the Reeds, were in a peculiarly distressing situation. They knew not whether their father was living or dead. No tidings had reached them since his letters ceased to be found by the wayside. The meat they had obtained from the Breen and Graves family was now gone, and on Christmas morning their breakfast was a "pot of glue," as the boiled rawhide was termed.

But Mrs. Reed, a tender-hearted mother, had a surprise in store this day for Virginia, Patty, James and Thomas. (Patty Reed, mentioned here, carried a doll with her through the ordeal. The story of *Patty Reed's doll*, written by author Rachel Laurgaard, has informed children about the Donner tragedy for decades. The doll itself is preserved for viewing at the Sutter Fort State Park in Sacramento, California.)

McGlashan writes, "When the last ox had been purchased, Mrs. Reed had placed the frozen meat in one corner of the cabin, so that pieces could be chipped off with a knife or hatchet. The tripe, however, she cleaned carefully, and hung on the outside of the cabin on the end of a log, close to the ground. She knew that the snow would soon conceal this from view. She also laid away secretly one teacupful of white beans, about half that quantity of rice, the same measure of dried apples, and a piece of bacon two inches square.

"She knew that if Christmas found them alive, they would be in a terribly destitute condition. She therefore resolved to lay these articles away, and to give them to her starving children for a Christmas dinner.

"This was done. The joy and gladness of these four little children knew no bounds when they saw the treasures unearthed and cooking on the fire. They were, just this one meal, to have all they could eat!

'They laughed, and danced, and cried by turns. They eagerly watched the dinner as it boiled. The pork and tripe had been cut in dice-like pieces. Occasionally one of these pieces would boil up to the surface of the water for an instant; then a bean would take a peep at them from the boiling kettle; then a piece of apple or a grain of rice. The appearance of each tiny bit was hailed by the children with shouts of glee.

"The mother, whose eyes were brimming with tears, watched her famished darlings with emotions

that can only be imagined. It seemed too sad that inno-
cent children should be brought to such destitution -
that the very sight of food should so affect them.

'When the dinner was prepared, the mother's
constant injunction was, "Children, eat slowly; there is
plenty for all." When they thought of the starvation of
tomorrow, they could not repress a shade of sadness,
and when the name of papa was mentioned all burst
into tears.

"Dear, brave papa! Was he struggling to relieve
his starving family, or lying stark and dead 'neath the
snows of the Sierra? This question was constantly up-
permost in the mother's mind."

Four different relief expeditions went to the rescue of the Donner party. Those who survived became
prominent in the history of California. The names of
Donner, Breen, Murphy, Foster, Graves, Reed, Eddy,
McCutcheon, and others of the party, are well known.

Donner Lake, calm and peaceful among the
sighing pines, is often the scene of some tourists'
camp. Relics of the days of '46 and '47 were found for
years after. One imagines that each mute piece had a
story of death and starvation hidden in it.

The travelers in trains, planes and motor vehicles who pass over the Sierra near Donner Lake, un-
mindful of the struggles of the Donner Party; see the
white peaks of snow on which rest the golden after-
glow of the sun, as the holy spires of God's eternal cathedrals, not as cold, menacing walls of entrapment

which they became for those early pioneers.

The pioneers fought their battles with the elements. Their names have been recorded in history. Let the names of the many unknown persons in unmarked graves be remembered for their bravery in their struggles to travel to new homes in the West. Let us cherish their heroic deeds and their strength.

Donner Lake in Winter

Stories from California's Colorful Past

The Bear Flag Republic

At sunrise on June 11, 1846, thirteen men left Fremont's camp at the Buttes, near the mouth of the Feather River. They were armed with rifles and pistols. They crossed the Sacramento River, and made their was to Gordon's Ranch, on Cache Creek.

Gordon gave the men a bullock, which they killed and roasted over a big fire. The men had a fine supper, then they traveled all night. The next day nineteen men joined them. They road down into the Sonoma Valley several nights later, and surrounded the Californios settlement, and captured the people living there. At this time the Mexicans were called the Californios, and the Eastern people who had settled in this land were Americans. Sonoma is a small town, but it has played an important part in the history of California. On June 14, 1846, there was a Mission, a few adobe houses, barracks, plaza, residence of General Vallejo, the house of Jacob Leese, which was used in after years as the headquarters of Colonel Joe Hooker, Major Phil Kearny, Captain Stoneman, Lieutenant Derby, and others known to fame.

At daybreak, on June 14th, thirty-three men surrounded Vallejo's house. He was roused from his bed and taken prisoner. He said: "I surrender, because I am without a force to defend me. I ask time to dress."

When he was told that no harm was intended, wine was given to the men. The men who went in to capture Vallejo stayed so long that those on the outside sent a man named William Ide to ascertain the cause of delay. He found that they were having a merry time. Ide came out and reported.

Then a demand was made that the prisoners be taken to Fremont camp in the Sacramento Valley. Grigsby, one of the men asked: "What are the orders of Fremont?" No one could answer. It seemed that no orders existed. A scene of wild confusion ensued. One swore he would not remain, another said, "We'll all have our throats cut."

There was a move to quit the scheme, when Ide stepped up and said; "The Californios have told us to leave or die. We must protect ourselves. I will not run, like a coward. If we do not succeed, we'll be nothing but robbers or horse thieves. We must succeed."

General Mariano Vallejo

The speech made the men rally around Ide, who was chosen the leader. "Now, take the fort!" he said. It was taken without a gun being fired, and the post at Sonoma was captured, with eighteen prisoners, nine brass cannon, two hundred and fifty guns, and a thousand dollars worth of property.

Vallejo and three other prisoners were sent to Fremont's camp. The first thing the Americans needed was a flag. It did not take long to produce one. A piece of coarse white cloth, about two yards long and one yard wide, was used. A narrow strip of red woolen stuff from an old flannel shirt was sewed on the edge.

"There ought to be a bear on the flag," said one of the men; and John Todd drew a large single star and a queer-shaped animal which he called a grizzly bear. Below the figures were the words: "California Republic."

The flag was then run up on the pole where before had floated the Mexican colors. Rules of order and discipline were adopted. Ide again made a speech, this time to the Californios, in which he said; "We do not intend to rob you or deprive you of liberty. We want equal justice for all men." It was the purpose of the republic to overthrow tyranny and work for the rights of all.

The first night, it was decided to issue a declaration of freedom. Ide had taught a village school in Ohio, and knew something of text-books and politics.

In the silent hours of the night, from one o'clock until four, he wrote the new declaration. It was written in the glow of enthusiasm.

The new republic was to have civil and religious liberty. It would foster industry, virtue, literature, commerce, farming and manufacture. It asked the favor of Heaven and the help and wisdom and good sense of the people of California.

Connected with the Republic were two terrible incidents: Two Americans, named Cowie and Fowler, were lassoed, dragged, tied to trees, and cut to pieces by their captors, apparently the Californios. This took place near the present town of Healdsburg.

The other event was the shooting of three Californios, who were captured by Ford. Papers were found in their boots which were to mislead the Americans. The men were shot, though they threw away their guns and begged for life.

Kit Carson, who has figured in the song and story of the West, was with the Americans when this occurred.

War was now in the air. Castro, a leader of the Mexicans, with an armed force, was on his way to recapture Sonoma; and it was said that he could put to death every man, woman and child, except Ide, who was to be tortured like a beast.

One night the little band of Americans who had taken over Sonoma, expected an attack. There was the tramp of horses. It was four o'clock - the darkest hour

- just before the dawn. Every man was at his post. The cannon were ready. The signal was that when Ide dropped his gun, the men were to fire.

Nearer and nearer came the tramp of soldiers. Ide, with a light in his eye, was about to drop his gun. The same moment Kit Carson's voice rang out, "My God, they are going to fire!" Then the shout, "'Tis Fremont! 'tis Fremont!" broke out in the fort, and Fremont came wildly dashing up.

Two days after his arrival the American Flag was raised at Monterey, and when the news reached Sonoma, the Bear Flag was hauled down and the Stars and Stripes run up.

The Bear-Flag revolution was at an end. Its flag was formerly in the Pioneer Hall, San Francisco, but was destroyed in the great fire of 1906.

The Bear Flag of the short lived Bear Flag Republic

Stories from California's Colorful Past

The American Flag in California

The story about raising the flag at the Golden Gate can be told in a few words. Away down the coast at Matzatlan was a war-ship, commanded by John D. Sloat. The sailors heard about the Mexicans fighting General Taylor over on the Rio Grande. They wanted to be a part of the fighting themselves.

In June, 1845, Sloat received from George Bancroft, Secretary of the Navy, a secret letter. The orders were to blockade the Mexican ports, but first to sail through the Golden Gate and take possession of the port of San Francisco. He was told to treat all the people of California in the most friendly manner possible.

On May 13, 1846, Bancroft wrote that Congress had declared war against Mexico, and ordered Sloat to take possession as once of San Francisco, Monterey, and as many other Mexican ports as he could. But of San Francisco he said: "Take it without fail." The ship sailed into the Bay of Monterey on the second of July. He soon learned about the Bear Flag Revolution. There were two English war-ships in the bay. He was afraid of them. It was several days before he decided to raise the American flag at Monterey.

Sloat said: "I'd rather be blamed for doing too much, than doing too little." He demanded the surrender of the Mexican fort, and was referred to General Castro. Two hundred and fifty men then marched up, and without the firing of a gun pulled down the Mexican flag and hoisted in its place "Old Glory". This was on the 6th of July 1846.

As it floated its starry folds to the breeze, the men gave a mighty cheer. Twenty-one guns were fired as a salute to the flag; and from that moment in law California came under the control of the United States.

Commodore Sloat said to the sailors: "Do not tarnish the hopes of bright success by doing any act that you'd be ashamed to acknowledge before your God or country. Treat the people friendly, and offer no insult or offense to any one, particularly women."

In a few days the American flag floated over Sutter's Fort, Sonoma, and Bodega Bay; and in the country, north and south, it was hailed with delight by American immigrants. It was on July 9, 1846, that Commodore Montgomery, with seventy men, marched to the plaza of San Francisco, then called Yerba Buena, and amid the cheers of the people hauled down the Mexican colors and raised our country's flag. On the same afternoon Lieutenant Missroon, with a few men, went to the fort at the Presidio. He found it deserted. The old Spanish cannon, cast several centuries ago, and some small iron guns, spiked and useless, were exposed to the weather. The adobe walls were crumbled and the tile roofs tumbled in.

"Old Glory" was hoisted on the ramparts, and has since kept a sleepless watch and ward over the Golden Gate.

The Discovery of Gold

Gold! Gold! Gold! Have you ever seen it in the sand or in the rocks? The first man to see gold in the sand of California was James W. Marshall. The story of how he found the yellow pebbles may interest you.

He had built houses, also saw-mills and grist mills. Lumber cost a lot in California at that time; so he though it would be a good scheme to build a saw-mill. He got John A Sutter, a Swiss who built Sutter's Fort (now a California State Park) to furnish him some money and food.

Marshall started off in search of a site upon which to build a mill. He found one on the north fork of the American River at a place now known as Co-loma. This also is now a State Park.

Ox-teams, carts, pack animals, tools and food were on the grounds in a few days, and the mill was up on the 15th of January, 1848. Sutter had furnished the money and Marshall the experience in building the mill.

◆　　◆　　◆　　◆　　◆

John Augustus Sutter was born in Baden, Switzerlsnf, February 15, 1803. He was the son of Swiss parents. He received a commission in the Bern, Switzerland Reserve Corps, and became a Lieutenant. Failing in business, he left his family, sailing to New York where he arrived in July, 1834, moving on to

Missouri. He joined a party of hunters and travelers, and, after making a tour of New Mexico, he went as far as Fort Vancouver. He sailed for the Sandwich Islands as they were then called, and from there to Sitka, then down the coast to San Francisco, then up the Sacramento River, where he built the stockade which afterwards became famous as Sutter's Fort. He became the owner of very valuable estates. He had a flour-mill that cost $25,000, a saw-mill $10,000, and thousands of cattle, sheep and hogs.

◆　　◆　　◆　　◆　　◆

Captain John A. Sutter

When James Marshall who was working on Sutter's Mill, had the mill ready to run, it was found that the ditch which was to lead the water to the wheel was not deep enough.

Marshall opened the flood-gates and let a big swift stream rush through to deepen the ditch. The water ran all night. In the morning he shut the gates, and went down to see the effect.

Although stories vary, some say that Marshall was alone on that first inspection of the mill race where the water had done its work. The swift current had dug out the side and the bottom, and spread at the end of the ditch a mass of sand and gravel. While looking at it, he saw beneath the water in the ditch some little yellow pebbles. He picked one up and looked at it closely. Marshall knew that gold was bright, heavy, and easily hammered. The substance he had in his hand was bright and heavy. He laid it down on one stone and took up another stone and hammered the yellow pebble into different shapes. The vision of millions did not immediately dawn upon him. He did not know that that little pebble would people the land and make California leap into greatness.

Marshall returned to the mill, and said to the man who was working at the wheel: "I have found it." "What is it? asked the man. "Gold," said Marshall. "Oh, no," said the man; "that cannot be."

Marshall held out his yellow pebble and said: "I know it to be nothing else."

The men about the mill had no doubt read about Sir Walter Raleigh having taken home to England a lot of yellow clay from Virginia, and had little faith in the discovery.

Marshall started for Sutter's Fort. He carried with him a number of nuggets in a little rag package. Taking Sutter aside where nobody else could hear or see them, Marshall showed him the small yellow lumps, and said: "It is gold." Sutter tested it, read articles on gold, weighed it, and said that Marshall was right, and that the lumps were real gold

Marshall started back in the rain. The great white rain of California came down, but he went right on. Sutter promised to visit the mill the next day. Marshall was so excited that he could not wait for him, and met him on the road that next day.

The flood-gates at the mill were turned on again, and Sutter picked up a lot of the yellow lumps which he afterwards had made into a ring on which were written these words:

"The First Gold Found in California, January, 1848."

Sutter wanted the discovery kept secret so that the men who were working for him on a mill near the fort would not leave him and go to start goldfields. It is said that a woman told the secret to a teamster, who, in turn, told Sam Brannan and Smith, merchants at Sutter's Fort.

These two men were instrumental in making the discovery of gold known to the world. One man, Sam Brannan, left Sacramento for San Francisco where he had extra editions of his newspaper printed and sent to New York. Another man, Thomas O. Larkin of San

Francisco, wrote a full account of the gold discovery which he sent to James Buchanan, then Secretary of State. President Polk called attention to the matter in his message to Congress, December 5, 1848.

Great excitement was aroused at once. Men left their stores, trades and professions and crowded into the gold fields. The whole country sounded with the sordid cry of "Gold, gold, gold!" Houses were left half-finished, fields half-planted, and newspapers stopped because the editors and printers had gone to the mines.

People came to California by the thousands - from all walks of life - in search of gold. In 1849, there came by sea about thirty-five thousand people, and across the plains about forty-five thousand people.

The coming of so many people in so brief a space of time to a new country created conditions that had not been seen before.

They laid the foundations of California, and gave it the name which it will always bear as the Golden State of the Union. The little lumps of gold grew to millions of dollars. James W. Marshall, the discoverer, lived to be an old man. The State gave him money in his old age and when he died, erected a monument to him. It stands at Coloma, near the site of the historic mill.

The California Legislature granted John Augustus Sutter a pension of $250 per month. In 1873, he moved to Lancaster, Pennsylvania. He died in Washington, D.C., June 17, 1880.

Sutter's Fort, one of the greatest early "American" landmarks of its day. In 1841, Captain John A. Sutter, an adventurous Swiss gentlemen and of extraordinary prominence in the "gold discovery period" of California, purchased the provisions and supplies of the Russian-America Fur Co., then in possession of a trading stations at Fort Ross. The Russians were being sharply watched by the Spanish Governors, and at last decided to relinquish their hold on California and return to Alaska. Captain Sutter moved the purchased Russian supplies to a place on the south bank of the Sacramento River, where he erected a stout fort and named the place New Helvetia, after his home. Switzerland. This fort was the first structure on the site of the present thriving city of Sacramento, now the Capital of California.

Who Named the Golden Gate

The entrance to the Bay of San Francisco has always been the delight of the poet. It has been pictured in various songs during the last 200 years.

The strait between the sea and the bay is beautiful. Mount Tamalpais stands on one side, Sutro Heights on the other, and the wild sea dashes its foam against the rugged rocks. It makes a picture worthy of the inspired fancy of the poet.

The view of the Golden Gate is always beautiful. As the sun dips into the sea and shines back through the Golden Gate the view is picture perfect.

The strait is one mile wide at its narrowest point, and five miles long from sea to bay.

John C. Fremont, in his book, "Memoirs of My Life," writes: "To this gate I gave the name of Chrysopylae, or Golden Gate, for the same reasons that the harbor of Byzantium (Constantinople or Istanbul) was named the Golden Horn (Chrysoceras)."

The name was suggested to him by the beauty of the sunset, the gate like entrance to the bay, and the value of the harbor for the commerce of the world. He put the name on the map that was sent to the Senate of the United States, in June 1848.

Stories from California's Colorful Past

The Story of Fremont

This adventurer was surveying in the Pacific coastal region for the United States Government, when the Bear Flag Revolt began. He was born in South Carolina during the War of 1812, of an old and honored French family.

He is said to have been a natural student and scholar, for we find him while yet a boy, teaching mathematics on a Government ship in Cuban waters. His studious and exact habits were rewarded with a lieutenant's commission; and we next find him busy surveying and making maps of the then uncertain line between his own country and Canada on the headwaters of our great rivers.

Thomas Hart Benton, the broad-minded and brave Senator of Missouri, had been a Colonel under General Jackson in the War of 1812 war with England; and it would seem he never quite laid down his sword, but kept his eye on the British lion to the north to the end of his life.

He soon took notice of the quiet energy, and scientific skill of young Fremont, far up in the then unknown wilderness of our Western frontier, and when the still boyish-looking lieutenant was called to Washington to report, the great Senator took him to his house.

There he met, loved, and married Benton's daughter, Jessie, one of the most beautiful and brilliant young women in all the world.

But there was brave and dangerous work to be done, and Fremont must be up and away. The great big paw of the British Lion was reaching down from Canada; it already was laid on Oregon, and was reaching on down to the Bay of San Francisco.

Benton stood up in his place in the Senate, time after time, and almost continually cried out, as he pointed beyond the Rocky Mountains; "Yonder in the west lies the Orient; yonder lies the path to India."

And so Fremont was sent to find the path, even before the honeymoon was well half over. He left his young wife at St. Louis, and there procured a cannon of Captain Robert E. Lee, afterwards the great General Lee, a true friend of Fremont, and pushed on before the snow and ice melted from the mountains.

And when it became known that he had taken a cannon with him, the President sent an order that he must not take the cannon, as his was a mission of peace. But Jessie opened the letter, and forgot to send it on for half a year! So her brave explorer was not left defenseless.

And what perils! One night, near the Modoc lava beds, more than a third of his force was killed or wounded; and but for Kit Carson, not a man of Fremont's would have been left alive in that hand to hand battle in the darkness.

Fremont reports that the arrows his attackers used

had steel points, and were supplied from a British trading-post at the mouth of the Umpqua River, Oregon. He adds: "Kit Carson says they are most warlike arrows he ever saw." The Athenaeum, an English authority of this time, said: "We are glad that Lieutenant Fremont has been sent to survey Oregon; for we know it will be well done, and we will then know how much blood and treasure to spend to secure that wild region."

Fremont led three of these daring expeditions, one after the other, in ensuing years. He named the Golden Gate long before gold was found, fought through the Mexican war, from Mount Shasta to Los Angeles, and then was elected one of the first two United States Senators from California.

Seldom had there been such an active person in our young nation's history. Fremont, like some other leaders, was always a student, a student from his cradle to his grave.

When others laughed or told stories of adventure around the camp or cabin fires, Fremont was in his tent or under a tree with his books. He knew every tree or plant. He could speak several languages.

Fremont was seen as a hero and had supporters from one end of the land to the other. In 1856 he ran for President.

In the fearful Civil War he was a conspicuous figure. Many who did not like Fremont, clamored for his retirement from the field of action, yet he could not be

John C. Fremont

idle for a day. He tried to worked for a railroad to California, but powerful men were against his plan. In fact, except for his fortunate marriage, Fremont was never the favorite of fortune. Despite his high offices and national renown, he died poor. Of his final hours (1890) let his sweet, gentle wife, Jessie, speak. She says:

"Of the many kindnesses unknown Fate reserved for Fremont, the kindest was the last. He had just succeeded in a most cherished wish. Peace and rest were again secured, when he was attacked in New York by what he thought was a passing summer illness. His physician recognized danger, and quickly the cessation of pain showed a fatal condition.

Night and day his loving son watched over him, and with their long-time friend and physician, kept unbroken his happy composure. Rousing from a prolonged, deep sleep the General said: "If I continue so comfortable I can finish my writing next week and go home." Seeing the eyes closing again, his physician said, to test the mind: "Home? Where do you call home, General?

"One last clear look, a pleased smile: 'California, of course.'"

Stories from California's Colorful Past

Who Named California?

California is mentioned for the first time, as far as anyone has been able to discover, in an old Spanish romance, *The Exploits of Esplandian*, first printed in 1510. The name appears in the following passages:

"Know that, on the right hand of the Indies, very near to the Terrestrial Paradise, there is an island called California, which was peopled with black women, without any men among them, because they were accustomed to live after the fashion of Amazons.

"In this island are many griffins, on account of the great savageness of the country and the immense quantity of wild game found there.

"Now, in the time that those great men of the Pagus sailed (against Constantinople), with those great fleets of which I have told you, there reigned in this land of *California* a queen, large of body, very beautiful, in the prime of her years," etc.

The name California next appears in the memoirs of the Conquistador Bernal Diaz del Castillo, who served with Cortez in the conquest of Mexico. He writes that "Cortez set sail from Santa Cruz, and discovered the coast of California."

The name of California was gradually used to designate the region from the Gulf of California to the mythical "Straits of Anian" which were very probably the Bering Straits.

The country was called "New Albion" by Sir

Francis Drake in 1579.

A paper published by the U.S. government in 1878, reported that the name California may have derived from the two Spanish words, caliente fornalla - "hot furnace" - was given by Cortez, in the year 1535, to the peninsula now known as Lower California, of which he was the discoverer, on account of its hot climate.

The region north of San Diego has long been called Alta California, and that to the south, Baja California. Several of the early Californios of Alta California, including the Vallejos, Alvarado, and others, agreed that the name came from Baja California natives. An early resident of Sinaloa, E. D. Guilbert informed Hubert Bancroft in 1878 that an old Indian of his locality called the peninsula (of Baja California) "Tchalifalnial" which sounded like "California" to those who heard the word.

Two Jesuit missionaries, Venegas and Clavigero believed that the discoverers had founded the name on these misunderstood words of the natives, or perhaps had made up the name from Latin or Greek. Bancroft gives as Greek *"kala phor nea"* which he translates as beautiful woman.

How California Came Into the Union

Now for a story that has no hero. The United States of America was at war with Mexico. What had been known as Alta California, and much other land, became part of the United States.

The people of Alta California wanted to form their own state, and so they held a convention at Monterey, September 1, 1849. A constitution was adopted, officers elected, and laws passed before California was admitted into the Union. The first Legislature met at San Jose. It passed many laws, and gave the names to the counties of the State. Fremont and Gwin were elected to become United States Senators. They went to Washington and asked that California be admitted to the Union. The President sent a special message to Congress about California.

There were some great speakers and powerful men on both sides of the issue of statehood for California. In the Senate, Clay, Calhoun, Webster, Seward and Jefferson Davis - men whom you will read about in the history of our country - were interested in California. Calhoun and Davis did not want California admitted because of the Slavery Question which divided the country in the years before the Civil War. Almost the last speech Calhoun made was against California. He thought it would bring trouble between the North and South. When he tried to talk he was too weak, and another Senator read his speech. It was an

Artful speech, and a great oration to those of the South. Daniel Webster answered it with his own great speech. Senator Webster said: "I believe in the Spartan maxim: "Improve, adorn what you have; seek no further." I do not fear slavery in California because the soil, climate, and everything connected with the region is opposed to slave labor. There has been talk of secession, peaceable secession. You might as well talk of a planet withdrawing from the solar system without a convulsion, as to talk about peaceable secession.

"The Union, which has been so hard to form, has linked together the destinies of all parts of the country, and has made a great nation, because it is a united nation, with a common name, and a common flag, and a common patriotism. It has conferred upon the South no less than upon the North great blessings.

"There may be violence; there may be revolution; the great dead may be disturbed in their graves.

"All this is possible, but not peaceable secession. The Union is one; it is a complete whole. It is bounded, like the buckler of Achilles, on either side by the ocean.

William H. Seward, another name that you will hear about in the history of our country, said: "California ought to be admitted at once; California comes from that clime where the West dies away into the rising East; California, which bounds the empire and the continent; California, the youthful queen of the Pacific, in robes of freedom, inlaid with gold, is doubly welcome!

"The Stars and Stripes should wave over its ports, or it will raise aloft a banner for itself. It would be no mean ambition if it became necessary for its own protection to found an independent nation on the Pacific.

"It is farther away than the old colonies from England; it is out of the reach of railroads; the prairies, the mountains, and the desert, and isthmus ruled by foreign powers, and a cape of storms are between it and the armies of the Union."

The delegates from California prepared a new address, in which they related in detail the claims of California to be admitted into the Union.

It seems strange now, when there is no longer any division between North and South, that Congress should hesitate to receive as part of the Union the Golden Land of the West.

The bill making California a State passed the Senate August 13, 1850. There were thirty-four Senators who voted for it, and eight against it. On September 7th, the bill was up for passage in the House of Representatives. There were several attempts to defeat it, but the bill was passed by one hundred and fifty-four in favor and fifty-six against.

The President, Millard Fillmore, signed the bill September 9, 1850. On that date, California became the thirty-first State - the thirty-first star in the flag, in order of date of admission, but the equal in other respects of the other States in the Union. California has contributed more than its share to the material and intellectual wealth of the world. Its treasures of gold, of soil, of climate; the patriotism of its citizens; the excellence of its universities, churches, and libraries; its spirit of progress, the friendly welcome it offers newcomers, its color and art atmosphere make California the ideal "Golden State."

President Millard Fillmore

The Story of the Great San Francisco Earthquake and Fire of 1906

The San Francisco fire of 1906 originated in an earthquake on April 18, 1906, affecting an area of 450 miles in length and 50 in width at most points.

Two thousand five hundred and ninety-three acres or 4.05 square miles were destroyed in the heart of downtown business and residence districts, about one-third of the city. Loss of life resulting from it was originally estimated at 452 people. (Current estimates are much higher.) Loss of property was $350,000,000 based on values at that time. 28,188 buildings were destroyed.

Another historic conflagration, the Great Chicago fire of 1871 destroyed 2,000 acres and 776 buildings, as a loss of $165,000,000.

The relative damage in this California earthquake was greater in some outlying towns, such as San Jose.

The new City Hall of San Francisco, after the 1906 earthquake and fire.

Failure of the water system caused a resort to dynamite to destroy buildings in the path of the flames to stop their progress.

Two hundred fifty thousand people were made homeless by the fire and many businesses were ruined.

Steel frame buildings, and those built on rock or with good foundations stood the shock and strain best. Steel and concrete construction was generally adopted in the rapid rebuilding, giving at least some security against a recurrence of the disaster.

* * * * *

Here is a personal account, written May 1, 1906: "The night of April 17, 1906 was beautiful. The stars hung low from a clear sky, the air was balmy. A wave of heat rippled into your face from the south. It was a strangely silent night. On my way home from the theatre to the Richmond District, San Francisco, I had a queer personal experience. A strange white dog with sore eyes, and pitifully poor, followed me to the house. The dog tried to express his desire for companionship and sympathy in the appealing gaze of his eyes. When the door of the house was opened, the dog rushed in, and began to bark, and then whine. A few hours after the dog was put out of the house, the earthquake came. The dog knew, as several birds knew, that the earth was out of tune. For several days many people testified that cats pussy-footed about, showing danger signals that were significant and mysterious. Horses and other animals were stamping in their stalls affrighted, several hours before the earthquake. So the white dog knew, and his piteous howling was almost human. It was more real than the cry of the banshee behind stage scenery, at a theatrical production. The earthquake came at 5:13 a.m. Wednesday morning, April 18, 1906. The earth lifted and went in a tremendous zigzag. Fabled Atlas, who had carried the globe on his shoulders, let it fall. Buildings fell, houses crumbled. Great steel beams were twisted. Chaos reigned. The house in which I lived was moved from its foundations; tables were overturned, glass broken. In the crash I landed on the floor on my back. My first thought was that the dog knew that the end of the world had come.

In a few minutes everybody was on the streets, thousands of people only partially dressed. The birds began to sing. The crash and roar of the ocean increased. The ambulances came. Express wagons, vehicles without regard to speed limits, wheelbarrows, baby carriages and trunks filled the streets. The sun came up and flooded the city with its brightness. Then the fire came. Smoke curled with picturesque effect from a hundred different places. The red tongues of flame reached towards the sky. I ran to the Lone Mountain, and from this resting place of the bones of the dead, I saw a great city on fire. For three days the city burned, and was destroyed, not by earthquake, but by fire. It is true that some poorly constructed building were wrecked, and thousands of brick chimneys collapsed from the shock. The loss would not have been great if the city had been able to stop the onward rush of the flames. Men and women rushed here and there as the city burned. The first thought was not for property, but for loved ones who might be killed or injured. The second thought was of valuable papers and records. The third thought was for personal safety. I was fortunate in securing a horse and buggy, and made a tour of the line of fire. The white heat, the red fire, and the black and gray smoke, were great. The fire fighters were brave, tireless and strong, but the fire was triumphant. The city was without light, water, sewers and a regular supply of food. There was no regular work for most people. Mayor Eugene Schmitz, with a vision greatly to his credit, ordered all saloons closed, all whisky destroyed, and free milk to be distributed for the children. A committee of fifty, and the State and National Governments responded to the call of the mayor, and order was restored.

Pliny the Younger, in describing the eruption of Vesuvius, which destroyed Pompeii, and in which the historian, the Elder Pliny lost his life, shows how history repeats itself. Here was the same motley crowd seeking safety in the parks, on the hills, vacant lots, and in flight to distant lands. A blind man sat a whole night and part of the day waiting for some one to take him to safety. Millionaires and day laborers, poets and butchers, members of all classes, neighbored together. At the ferry, the wild rush to get across was on. Men, women and children were there, loaded with blankets, bird cages, parrots, and both valuable and valueless household articles. They had struggled from street to street, avoiding the places where the flames burned the fiercest.

A caravan of people moved out Mission Street. Everybody was loaded with personal belongings, the fire licking at their heels. There were many people pulling trunks along the sidewalks, vehicles of all sorts carrying an old portrait of some dear ancestor, or perhaps some object of no value whatever. It was but the weak attempt to save something from the fire. In times of great stress the little things are of as much importance as the big things. The exodus was a thrilling sight. It meant that over 200,000 people were homeless. A hundred thousand were in the parks. Rumors of approaching flames would drive many into wild hysterics. In many cases the people would not leave their homes until the flames came into the back or front doors. There were few tears, and much heroic work. Those who remained in the city cooked in the streets, in the backyards, slept out of doors in tents or temporary cabins. The officials devoted themselves to the sanitary conditions. The weeks so passed. The people began to smile at misfortune and to actually enjoy the life out of doors. The great earthquake and fire banished selfishness. When the people of other cities sent millions, emotion was strained to tears. The awful desolation and the new, clean poverty of the people was hid by the hand of friendliness over the eyes of the refugees; while fraternities with secret oaths to help a brother, churches with creeds, citizens in fierce competition, all responded to the call of brotherhood as wide as humanity itself. It was the Sermon on the Mount in action.

There would be a new San Francisco, a greater San Francisco. The fire was a catastrophe that struck the city on that April morning but the new city shall become a wonder of the Twentieth century - new schools, new churches, new public service utilities, new honor and fame - new, new everything new.

(Written May 1, 1906 - anonymous)

Facts about California:
(As adopted by the California Legislature)
Nickname: Golden State
State Capital: Sacramento
State Color: Blue and Gold
Flower: Golden poppy
Animal: California Grizzly Bear (Ursus Californicus
Marine Mammal: California Gray Whale (Eshrichtius Robustus)
Bird: California Valley Quail (Lophortyx Californica)
Tree: Redwood
Fish: Golden Trout (Salmo Agua-bonita)
Marine Fish: Garibaldi (Hypsypops Rubicundus)
Fossil: Sabre-tooth cat (Smilodon Californicus)
Insect: California Dogface Butterfly (Zerene Eurydice)
Mineral: Gold
Gemstone: Benitoite
Rock: Serpentine
Prehistoric Artifact: Chipped Stone Bear (From San Diego County)
Reptile: Desert Tortoise (Gopherus Agassizi)
Geography:
Highest Point: Mt. Whitney, 14,494 feet
Lowest Point: Death Valley, 282 feet below sea level
Size: 163,707 square miles, 3rd largest state

The Great Seal of the State of California

In the Seal of the State of California is Minerva, with the Golden Gate, a bear, and a ship in full sail in the bay. A Miner is at work. Sierra Nevada Mountains are in the background. The State Motto is written in the upper portion of the Seal. Eureka means, "I have found it."

The score to the California State Song, *I Love You, California* is reproduced on the following pages
I Love You, California -
available on audio tape from
James Stevenson Publisher as
arranged and performed by Cathrael Hackler
and John Foster.

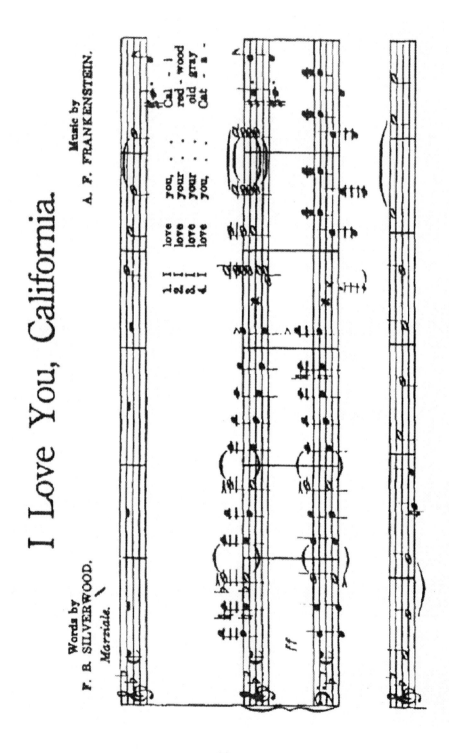

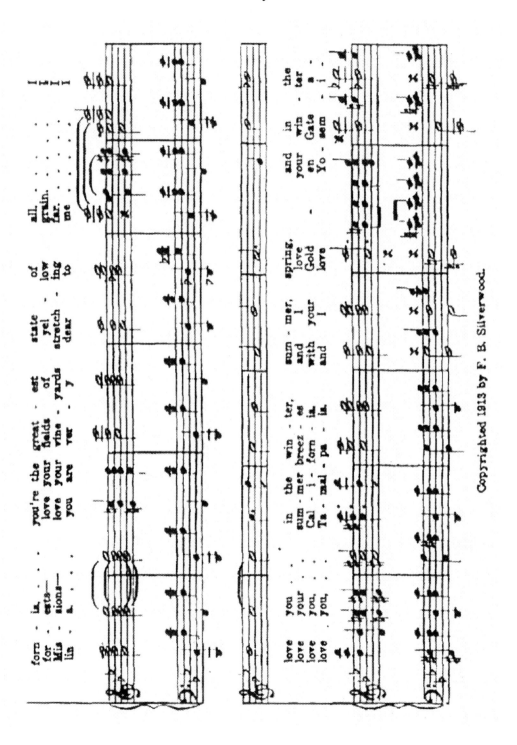

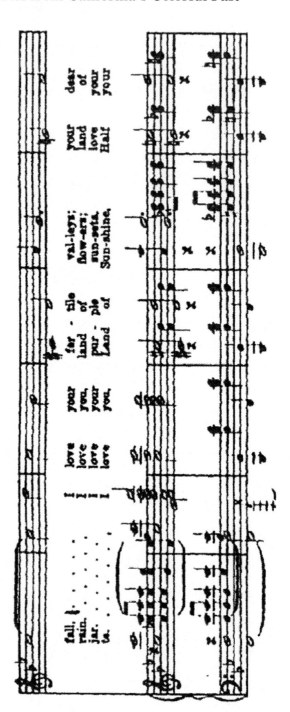

I Love You California

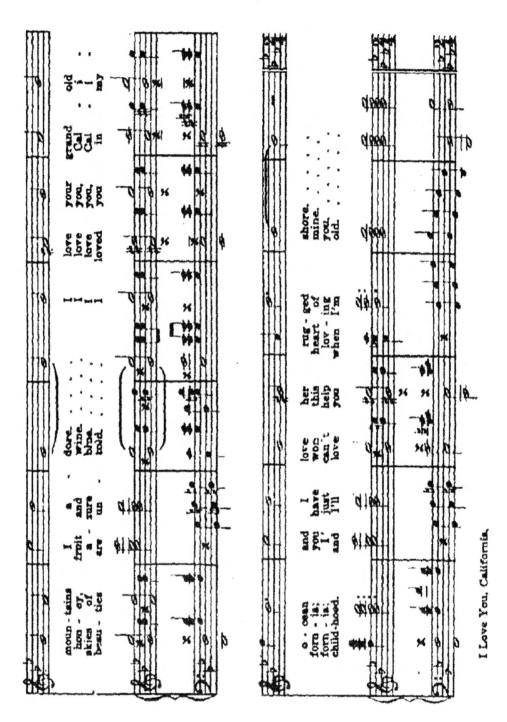

I Love You, California

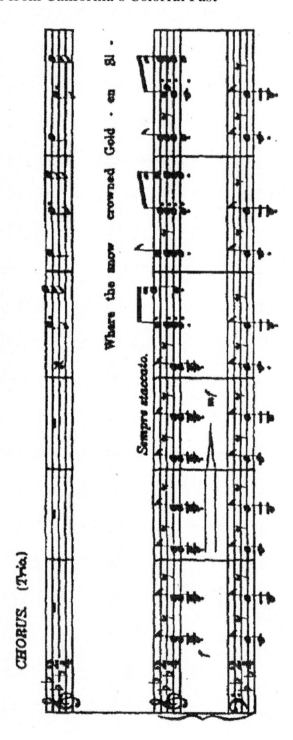

I Love You, California.

I Love You California

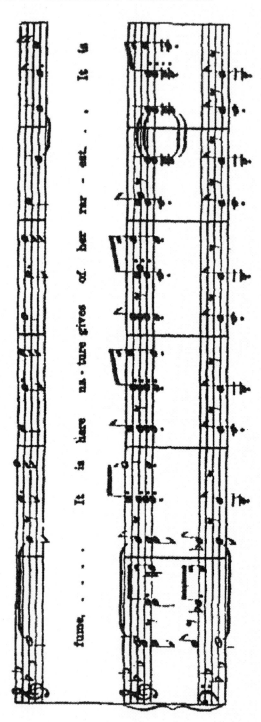

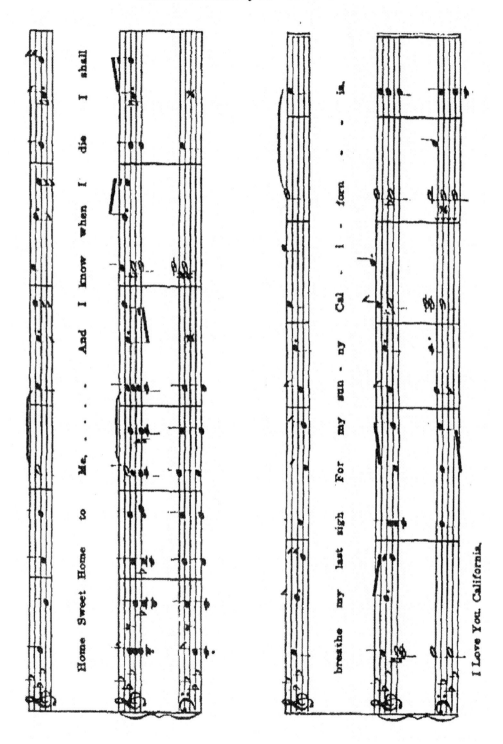

Bret Harte poem, at Mission Delores, 1868
"Angelus"

Bells of the Past, whose long -forgotten music
Still fills the wide expanse,
Tingeing the sober twilight of the present
With the color of Romance!

I hear your call, and see the sun descending
On rock and wave and sand,
As down the coast the mission voices, blending,
Girdle the Indian land.

Within the circle of your incantation
No blight nor mildew falls;
Nor fierce unrest, nor lust, nor low ambition
Passes those airy walls.

Borne on the swell of your long waves receding,
I touch the farther past -
I see the dying glow of Spanish glory,
The sunset dream and last!

Before me rise the dome-shaped mission towers,
The white Presidio;
The swart commander in his leather jacket,
The priest in stole of snow.

Once more I see Portola's cross uplifting
Above the setting sun;
And past the headland, northward, slowly drifting,
The freighted galleon.

O solemn bells! whose consecrated masses
Recall the faith of old,
O tinkling bells, that lulled with twilight music -
The spiritual fold!

Your voices break and falter in the darkness,
Break, falter, and are still.
And veiled and mystic, like the Host descending,
The sun sinks from the hill!

**California History books by
James Stevenson Publisher
1500 Oliver Road, Suite K-109
Fairfield, CA 94533
(707) 208-2756 or Fax (206) 350-2954
http://jspub.com/bookcat.htm**

*California Missions: History and Model Building
Ideas for Children*

*Stowaway to California! Adventures with Father
Serra*

Captain Sutter's Fort, Adventures with John A. Sutter

*California's Beginnings, A Children's Reader
(stories from California's days under Mexican and
Spanish rule)*

The Capital That Couldn't Stay Put—award winning
book about the Capital of California from its earliest
days through various refurbishing efforts

Joe's Luck, A Horatio Alger classic about an orphan
boy who succeeds through hard work

Humbugs and Heroes
A comprehensive write-up of California's Frauds and
Heroes

The Story of the Pony Express, A Concise History
Includes unpublished material on an occasionally used
route from Sacramento overland to San Francisco

CPSIA information can be obtained at www.ICGtesting.com
Printed in the USA
267475BV00002B/27/A